CAT Wit

QUIPS AND QUOTES FOR THE FELINE-OBSESSED

KATE MAY

summersdale

CONTENTS

EDITOR'S NOTE

For nearly 10,000 years cats have been driving us crazy. They were worshipped in ancient Egypt, and, as P. G. Wodehouse pointed out, they have never forgotten this. If you think cats don't care about us though, think again: as Michael Nelson noted, they have a knack of knowing what time we have to be up in the morning – and waking us up twenty minutes before the alarm goes off.

Humans have been finding felines funny since long before the days of YouTube videos. Cats may be aloof and clever, but they're also unbelievably cute. From Cervantes to Dickens, there have always been people who agree with Robert A. Heinlein, who said that 'There is no such thing as "just a cat".'

We endure the scratches, the snootiness and the various 'presents' left by our mangy moggies, perfect purebreds, cuddly kittens and wise old cats because deep down we know that all these slights are a small price to pay for the pleasure of cohabiting with these elegant creatures. And there's nothing quite like the purr-fect affection of a cat.

So why not sit back with your feline friend in your lap and celebrate all the reasons you love them, with this witty collection of quips and quotes on the joys, trials and delights of your favourite household deity, the cat.

LOVE ME, LOVE MY CAT

Since each of us is
blessed with only
one life, why not
live it with a cat?

ROBERT STEARNS

No heaven will not ever heaven be;
Unless my cats are there
to welcome me.

ANONYMOUS

———•●•———

Time spent with cats
is never wasted.

SIGMUND FREUD

———•●•———

There are two means of
refuge from the miseries
of life: music and cats.

ALBERT SCHWEITZER

Wherever a cat sits, there
shall happiness be first.

STANLEY SPENCER

———•●•———

His attitude seemed to be, how
can anyone not love a cat?

VICKI MYRON

———•●•———

If I tried to tell you how
much I love my cats, you
wouldn't believe me.

LEXIE SAIGE

Only cat lovers know the luxury of fur-coated, musical hot-water bottles that don't go cold.

SUZANNE MILLEN

Animals are such agreeable
friends – they ask no questions,
they pass no criticisms.

GEORGE ELIOT

———•●•———

Getting a cat is a
greater commitment than
getting married.

SEYMOUR CHWAST AND PAULA SCHER

It often happens
that a man is more
humanely related to
a cat or dog than to
any human being.

HENRY DAVID THOREAU

WHAT A BEAUTIFUL PUSSY YOU ARE!

Two things are
aesthetically perfect
in the world – the
clock and the cat.

ÉMILE-AUGUSTE CHARTIER

Class she certainly was,
from her tapered black head,
beautiful as an Egyptian queen
carved out of ebony, to the tip
of her elegant whip tail.

DOREEN TOVEY

———•••———

Cats never strike a pose
that isn't photogenic.

LILIAN JACKSON BRAUN

God made the cat in
order that man might
have the pleasure of
caressing the lion.

FERNAND MÉRY

How could I help but be smitten
with his scraggly little blackness…

PATRICIA KHULY

———•●———

I think it's the fact that they have
to spend a good part of the day
putting their hair back in place.

DEBBIE PETERSON ON WHY CATS DISLIKE BATHS

———•●———

Cats sleep fat and walk thin.

ROSALIE MOORE

A thing of beauty, strength,
and grace lies behind
that whiskered face.

ANONYMOUS

Her function is to sit
and be admired.

GEORGINA STRICKLAND GATES

The Owl looked up to
the stars above,
And sang to a small guitar,
'O lovely Pussy! O Pussy, my love,
What a beautiful Pussy you are…'

EDWARD LEAR, FROM 'THE OWL AND THE PUSSYCAT'

WHY CATS ARE BETTER THAN DOGS

I used to love dogs
until I discovered cats.

NAFISA JOSEPH

Dogs come when they're
called; cats take a message
and get back to you later.

MARY BLY

———————•●•———————

A dog will flatter you but you
have to flatter the cat.

GEORGE MIKES

———————•●•———————

If animals could speak, the
dog would be a blundering
outspoken fellow; but the cat
would have the rare grace of
never saying a word too much.

MARK TWAIN

Your cat will never threaten
your popularity by barking
at three in the morning.

HELEN POWERS

———— •●• ————

Dogs have owners,
cats have staff.

ANONYMOUS

———— •●• ————

Even the stupidest cat seems
to know more than any dog.

ELEANOR CLARK

Cats are smarter than dogs.
You can't get eight cats to
pull a sled through snow.

JEFF VALDEZ

●●●

The cat is a character of being;
the dog is a character of doing.

MICHAEL J. ROSEN

You can tell a dog to
do something. You
can put it to a cat as a
reasonable proposition.

MICHAEL STEVENS

The one disservice animals render us is that they don't live as long as we do. But cats live longer than dogs.

DOREEN TOVEY

Dogs are eternally grateful that humans exist; cats, however, are simply mildly appreciative!

CARL BRIZZI

WHO'S BOSS?

A cat chooses its
owner, not the other
way around.

HELEN BROWN

If he is asleep in the middle of
the bed when it's time for my
day to end, I sleep curled up
in a corner of the mattress.

PETER GETHERS

⸺●●●⸺

When cats leap onto your bed, it's
because they adore your bed.

ALISHA EVERETT

⸺●●●⸺

Women and cats will do as they
please, and men and dogs should
relax and get used to the idea.

ANONYMOUS

If man could be crossed with the cat it would improve the man, but it would deteriorate the cat.

MARK TWAIN

———————●●●———————

The dog may be wonderful prose, but only the cat is poetry.

FRENCH PROVERB

———————●●●———————

Cat's motto: no matter what you've done wrong, always try to make it look like the dog did it.

ANONYMOUS

Cats' hearing apparatus
is built to allow
the human voice to
easily go in one ear
and out the other.

STEPHEN BAKER

The key to a successful new relationship between a cat and human is patience.

SUSAN EASTERLY

———•●•———

Every dog has his day – but the nights are reserved for the cats.

ANONYMOUS

———•●•———

One reason we admire cats is for their proficiency in one-upmanship. They always seem to come out on top.

BARBARA WEBSTER

THE PITTER PATTER OF TINY PAWS

A kitten is chiefly
remarkable for rushing
about like mad at
nothing whatever, and
generally stopping
before it gets there.

AGNES REPPLIER

He raised his head and emitted an impressive yowl for a creature only four inches in length, tip-to-tail.

PATRICIA KHULY

A kitten is the delight of the household; all day long a comedy is played out by an incomparable actor.

CHAMPFLEURY

Nothing's more playful than a young cat, nor more grave than an old one.

THOMAS FULLER

Kittens can happen to anyone.

PAUL GALLICO

The playful kitten with its
pretty little tigerish gambol is
infinitely more amusing than
half the people one is obliged
to live with in the world.

SYDNEY, LADY MORGAN

There is no more
intrepid explorer
than a kitten.

CHAMPFLEURY

A kitten... does not discover
that her tail belongs to her
until you tread on it.

HENRY DAVID THOREAU

———•●•———

A beating heart and an angel's
soul, covered in fur.

LEXIE SAIGE

———•●•———

It is a very inconvenient habit
of kittens (Alice had once made
the remark) that, whatever you
say to them, they always purr.

LEWIS CARROLL

THE HUNTER

The cat does not
negotiate with
the mouse.

ROBERT K. MASSIE

The clever cat eats
cheese and breathes
down rat holes with
baited breath.

W. C. FIELDS

A cat brings you gifts: half a
lizard, an eviscerated squirrel,
but she means well.

LEONORE FLEISCHER

———— •●• ————

Cats too, with what silent
stealthiness, with what light steps
do they creep towards a bird!

PLINY

———— •●• ————

The cat loves fish, but she's
loath to wet her feet.

PROVERB

When she walked abroad she stretched out long and thin like a little tiger, and held her head high to look over the grass as if she were threading the jungle.

SARAH ORNE JEWETT

———•••———

Solomon grabbed the mouse and eyed us direly. Playing dramatically up to the role of a Panther Retreating With His Quarry...

DOREEN TOVEY

———•••———

Did St Francis preach to the birds? If he really liked birds... better to preach to the cats.

REBECCA WEST

A cat bitten once by a
snake dreads even rope.

ARAB PROVERB

———●●———

The cat in gloves catches no mice.

BENJAMIN FRANKLIN

———●●———

Cats of good breed hunt
better fat than lean.

BENVENUTO CELLINI

———●●———

A cat's idea of a 'good time'
is to kill something.

ANDY ROONEY

HOW TO SPEAK CAT

Cats speak a subtle language in which few sounds carry many meanings, depending on how they are sung or purred.

VAL SCHAFFNER

My cat speaks sign
language with her tail.

ROBERT A. M. STERN

If a cat spoke, it would say
things like, 'Hey, I don't
see the problem here.'

ROY BLOUNT JR

———•●•———

A cat can purr its way
out of anything.

DONNA MCCROHAN

———•●•———

A meow massages the heart.

STUART MCMILLAN

Meow is like aloha – it
can mean anything.

HANK KETCHUM

———•●●———

The purr from cat to man says,
'You bring me happiness;
I am at peace with you.'

BARBARA L. DIAMOND

———•●●———

If we treated everyone we
meet with the same affection
we bestow upon our favourite
cat, they, too, would purr.

MARTIN BUXBAUM

An animal's eyes have the power
to speak a great language.

MARTIN BUBER

An animal's eyes have the power
to speak a great language.

Could the purr be anything
but contemplative?

IRVING TOWNSEND

To err is human, to purr is feline.

ROBERT BYRNE

BEWARE OF THE CAT

Some people say man
is the most dangerous
animal on the planet.
Obviously those
people have never
met an angry cat.

LILLIAN JOHNSON

Those who'll play with cats
must expect to be scratched.

MIGUEL DE CERVANTES

———————●●●———————

People who hate cats will come
back as mice in their next life.

FAITH RESNICK

———————●●●———————

Much ceremony must be
observed, and a number of
diplomatic feelers put out, before
establishing a state of truce.

LLOYD ALEXANDER ON MAKING FRIENDS WITH HOMELESS CATS

Cat lovers can readily be
identified... their clothes always
look old and well used.

ERIC GURNEY

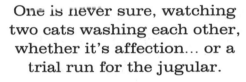

One is never sure, watching
two cats washing each other,
whether it's affection... or a
trial run for the jugular.

HELEN THOMSON

The cat that is kissing you lovingly
has just devoured a rabbit and has
left the entrails under the bed.

ANONYMOUS

I have an Egyptian cat.
He leaves a pyramid
in every room.

RODNEY DANGERFIELD

A tomcat has it so easy, he has only to spray and his presence is there for years on rainy days.

ALBERT EINSTEIN

———●●———

Lettin' the cat out of the bag is a whole lot easier 'n puttin' it back in.

WILL ROGERS

———●●———

It is better to cut off the sleeve of your best robe than to disturb a sleeping cat.

MUHAMMAD

Cats aren't clean, they're just covered with cat spit.

JOHN S. NICHOLS

———————●●●———————

No amount of masking tape can ever totally remove [a cat's] fur from your couch.

LEO DWORKEN

THE CAT'S PYJAMAS

Until one has loved
an animal, a part of
one's soul remains
unawakened.

ANATOLE FRANCE

Cats are intended to teach
us that not everything in
nature has a purpose.

GARRISON KEILLOR

Everything a cat is and does
physically is to me beautiful,
lovely, stimulating, soothing,
attractive and an enchantment.

PAUL GALLICO

If you are worthy of its
affection, a cat will be your
friend, but never your slave.

THÉOPHILE GAUTIER

Two cats can live as cheaply
as one, and their owner
has twice as much fun.

LLOYD ALEXANDER

———•••———

For me, one of the pleasures
of cats' company is their
devotion to bodily comfort.

COMPTON MACKENZIE

———•••———

A cat is the only domestic
animal I know who toilet trains
itself and does a damned
impressive job of it.

JOSEPH EPSTEIN

A cat improves the garden
wall in sunshine, and the
hearth in foul weather.

JUDITH MERKLE RILEY

———————•●•———————

Everything I know I learned
from my cat: When you're
hungry, eat. When you're
tired, nap in a sunbeam.

GARY SMITH

———————•●•———————

Cats are creatures that express a
multitude of moods and attitudes.

KAREN BRADEMEYER

There is nothing sweeter than
his peace when at rest.
For there is nothing brisker
than his life when in motion.

CHRISTOPHER SMART

———•●•———

It is a philosophic animal...
one that does not place its
affections thoughtlessly.

THÉOPHILE GAUTIER

MOGGY MAGIC

It always gives me a
shiver when I see a
cat seeing what
I can't see.

ELEANOR FARJEON

Their eyes are fathomless
depths of cat-world mysteries.

LESLEY ANNE IVORY

———————•●•———————

It's funny how dogs and cats
know the inside of folks better
than other folks do, isn't it?

ELEANOR H. PORTER

———————•●•———————

Cats look beyond appearances
– beyond species entirely, it
seems – to peer into the heart.

BARBARA L. DIAMOND

I love cats because I enjoy my home; and little by little, they become its visible soul.

JEAN COCTEAU

———●●●———

It has been the providence of Nature to give this creature nine lives instead of one.

VISHNU SHARMA

When they are among
us, cats are angels.

GEORGE SAND

Cats are magical... the more you
pet them the longer you both live.

ANONYMOUS

• ● •

All cats can see futures, and
see echoes of the past.

NEIL GAIMAN

• ● •

The cat is the mirror of
his human's mind.

WINIFRED CARRIÈRE

For the cat is cryptic,
and close to strange
things which men
cannot see.

H. P. LOVECRAFT

PURR-FECT PITCH

If there were to be
a universal sound
depicting peace, I would
surely vote for the purr.

BARBARA L. DIAMOND

A cat can be trusted to purr when
she is pleased, which is more than
can be said for human beings.

WILLIAM RALPH INGE

———●●●———

It was difficult to feel vexed
by a creature that burst
into a chorus of purring.

PHILIP BROWN

———●●●———

Are we really sure the purring
is coming from the kitty and
not from our very own hearts?

TERRI GUILLEMETS

No one shall deny me my
own conclusions, nor my
cat her reflective purr.

IRVING TOWNSEND

—••—

Purring would seem to be,
in her case, an automatic
safety valve device for dealing
with happiness overflow.

MONICA EDWARDS

—••—

Even if you have just destroyed
a Ming vase, purr. Usually
all will be forgiven.

LENNY RUBENSTEIN

When the tea is
brought at five o'clock
And all the neat
curtains are drawn
with care,
The little black cat
with bright green eyes
Is suddenly
purring there.

HAROLD MONRO, 'MILK FOR THE CAT'

If purring could be encapsulated, it'd be the most powerful antidepressant on the pharmaceutical market.

TERRI GUILLEMETS

A CAT MAY LOOK
AT A KING

The reason cats climb
is so that they can
look down on almost
every other animal.

K. C. BUFFINGTON

Thou art indeed...
the Great Cat.

PART OF THE INSCRIPTION ON THE ROYAL TOMBS AT THEBES

———•●●•———

In tho boginning, God created
man, but seeing him so feeble,
He gave him the cat.

WARREN ECKSTEIN

———•●●•———

Cats always know whether
people like or dislike them.
They do not always care enough
to do anything about it.

WINIFRED CARRIÈRE

When I play with my cat, who knows if I am not a pastime to her more than she is to me?

MICHEL DE MONTAIGNE

Cats conspire to keep us at arm's length.

FRANK PERKINS

In a cat's eye, all things belong to cats.

ENGLISH PROVERB

If cats could talk,
they wouldn't.

NAN PORTER

———•●•———

To respect the cat is the beginning
of the aesthetic sense.

ERASMUS DARWIN

———•●•———

The domestic cat seems to
have greater confidence in
itself than in anyone else.

LAWRENCE N. JOHNSON

A cat cares for you only as
a source of food, security,
and a place in the sun.

CHARLES HORTON COOLEY

———•●•———

As every cat owner knows,
nobody owns a cat.

ELLEN PERRY BERKELEY

CAT NAPS

Cats sleep anywhere,
any table, any chair...

ELEANOR FARJEON

One of the ways in which cats
show happiness is by sleeping.

CLEVELAND AMORY

———•••———

Laziness is nothing more
than the habit of resting
before you get tired.

JULES RENARD

———•••———

Most beds sleep up to six cats.
Ten cats without the owner.

STEPHEN BAKER

No day is so bad it can't
be fixed with a nap.

CARRIE SNOW

———•●•———

Cats, I reckon, have it all –
admiration and an endless
sleep, and company only
when they want it.

ROD MCKUEN

———•●•———

All cats love a cushioned couch.

THEOCRITUS

If there is one spot of
sun spilling onto the
floor, a cat will find
it and soak it up.

JOAN ASPER MCINTOSH

All of the animals except for man know that the principle business of life is to enjoy it.

SAMUEL BUTLER

•●•

Cats are rather delicate creatures... but I never heard of one who suffered from insomnia.

JOSEPH WOOD KRUTCH

•●•

[A cat is] a dreamer whose philosophy is sleep and let sleep.

SAKI

A little drowsing cat is an
image of perfect beatitude.

CHAMPFLEURY

The real measure of a day's heat
is the length of a sleeping cat.

CHARLES J. BRADY

You can't look at a sleeping
cat and be tense.

JANE PAULEY

'You are getting
very sleepy' is not
a command when
said to a cat; it is
an eternal truth.

ARI RAPKIN

FELINE FRIENDS

The cat could very
well be man's best
friend but would never
stoop to admitting it.

DOUG LARSON

We entertain a cat – he adorns
our hearth as a guest, fellow-
lodger, and equal because
he wishes to be there.

H. P. LOVECRAFT

The difference between friends
and pets is that friends we
allow into our company, pets
we allow into our solitude.

ROBERT BRAULT

Cats are distant, discreet,
impeccably clean and able to
stay silent. What more could be
needed to be good company?

MARIE LECZINSKA

Some people are born into
cat-loving families, some
achieve cats, and some have
cats thrust upon them.

WILLIAM H. A. CARR

You can tell your cat anything
and he'll still love you.

HELEN POWERS

When a cat chooses to be
friendly, it's a big deal,
because a cat is picky.

MIKE DUPREE

There are few things in life
more heart-warming than
to be welcomed by a cat.

TAY HOHOFF

How we behave toward
cats here below determines
our status in heaven.

ROBERT A. HEINLEIN

Beware of people who dislike cats.

IRISH PROVERB

A cat's name may
tell you more about
its owners than it
does about the cat.

LINDA W. LEWIS

I have found my love
of cats most helpful in
understanding women.

JOHN SIMON

Who hath a better
friend than a cat?

WILLIAM HARDWIN

THE QUALITIES OF CATS

There is, indeed,
no single quality
of the cat that man
could not emulate
to his advantage.

CARL VAN VECHTEN

Are cats lazy? Well, more
power to them if they are.

FERNAND MÉRY

———•●•———

To understand a cat, you
must realise that he has his
own gifts, his own viewpoint,
even his own morality.

LILIAN JACKSON BRAUN

———•●•———

The smart cat doesn't
let on that he is.

H. G. FROMMER

There are no ordinary cats.

COLETTE

—————•●•—————

With the qualities of cleanliness, affection, patience, dignity, and courage that cats have, how many of us, I ask you, would be capable of becoming cats?

FERNAND MÉRY

—————•●•—————

The cat is above all things, a dramatist.

MARGARET BENSON

A cat doesn't really need to know
that everybody loves him.

WILLIAM KUNSTLER

A dog is a man's best friend.
A cat is a cat's best friend.

ROBERT J. VOGEL

Curiosity is the very basis of
education and if... curiosity
killed the cat, I say only
the cat died nobly.

ARNOLD EDINBOROUGH

I have studied many philosophers and many cats. The wisdom of cats is infinitely superior.

HIPPOLYTE TAINE

Way down deep, we're all motivated by the same urges. Cats have the courage to live by them.

JIM DAVIS

If having a soul means being able to feel love and loyalty and gratitude, then animals are better off than a lot of humans.

JAMES HERRIOT

[Cats] have never completely got over the snootiness caused by that fact that in ancient Egypt they were worshipped as gods.

P. G. WODEHOUSE

HOUSE TRAINING

A cat is there when
you call her – if she
doesn't have something
better to do.

BILL ADLER

I had been told that the training
procedure with cats was difficult...
Mine had me trained in two days.

BILL DANA

———•●•———

Never try to out-stubborn a cat.

ROBERT A. HEINLEIN

———•●•———

There is no snooze button on
a cat who wants breakfast.

ANONYMOUS

Cats seem to go on the
principle that it never
does any harm to ask
for what you want.

JOSEPH WOOD KRUTCH

Essentially, you do not
so much teach your
cat as bribe him.

LYNN HOLLYN

A plate is distasteful to a cat,
a newspaper still worse; they
like to eat sticky pieces of
meat sitting on a cushioned
chair or a nice Persian rug.

MARGARET BENSON

———•••———

To a cat, 'NO!' means 'Not
while I'm looking.'

ANONYMOUS

———•••———

Can they be thinking,
'I'll be nice, and maybe she
will feed me twice?'

BETTE MIDLER

You can keep a dog; but it
is the cat who keeps people,
because cats find humans
useful domestic animals.

GEORGE MIKES

———————•••———————

Cats don't like change
without their consent.

ROGER CARAS

———————•••———————

You can't force it to come
to you and you can't force
it to stay with you.

PIERRE FOGLIA ON HOW A CAT IS LIKE HAPPINESS

Cats can be very funny,
and have the oddest
ways of showing they're
glad to see you.

W. H. AUDEN

CLEVER CATS

Cats are a mysterious
kind of folk. There
is more passing in
their minds than
we are aware of.

WALTER SCOTT

Cats always seem so very
wise, when staring with
their half-closed eyes.

BETTE MIDLER

———◆●◆———

Cats are independent, by
which I mean smart.

DAVE BARRY

———◆●◆———

Intelligence in the cat
is underrated.

LOUIS WAIN

As anyone who has ever been around a cat... knows, cats have enormous patience with the limitations of the human kind.

CLEVELAND AMORY

It was not I who was teaching my cat to gather rosebuds, but she who was teaching me.

IRVING TOWNSEND

Cats are smart. You know it and I know it.

DEBBIE MERTENS

The cat alone attains to the contemplative life. He regards the wheel of existence from without, like the Buddha.

ANDREW LANG

His intelligence keeps him
from doing many of the fool
things that complicate life.

CARL VAN VECHTEN

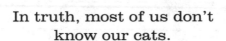

In truth, most of us don't
know our cats.

ELIZABETH MARSHALL THOMAS

Do not meddle in the affairs of
cats, for they are subtle and
will pee on your computer.

BRUCE GRAHAM

GLAMOUR PUSSES

There's no need for a
piece of sculpture in a
home that has a cat.
WESLEY BATES

A cat is a dilettante in fur.

THÉOPHILE GAUTIER

———•••———

A cat pours his body on
the floor like water. It is
restful just to see him.

WILLIAM LYON PHELPS

———•••———

Even overweight cats instinctively
know the cardinal rule: when fat,
arrange yourself in slim poses.

JOHN WEITZ

Which is more beautiful – feline movement or feline stillness?

ELIZABETH HAMILTON

———————●●●———————

Cats are living adornments.

EDWIN LENT

———————●●●———————

Cats assume their strangest, most intriguing and beautiful postures only when it is impossible to photograph them.

J. R. COULSON

The smallest feline
is a masterpiece.

LEONARDO DA VINCI

I thought she was the loveliest
animal I had ever seen.

DOREEN TOVEY

———•●•———

There is no such thing
as 'just a cat'.

ROBERT A. HEINLEIN

———•●•———

It is with the approach of winter
that cats... wear their richest fur
and assume an air of sumptuous
and delightful opulence.

PIERRE LOTI

The cat is the animal
to whom the Creator
gave the biggest
eye, the softest fur,
the most supremely
delicate nostrils.

COLETTE

AIN'T MISBEHAVIN'

I don't know he's
there until I yawn
and my mouth closes
on a whisker.

ASTRID ALAUDA ON THE CAT THAT CURLS
UP ON HER PILLOW IN THE NIGHT

Ignorant people think it is the
noise which fighting cats make
that is so aggravating, but
it ain't so; it is the sickening
grammar that they use.

MARK TWAIN

———————•••———————

Anything not nailed
down is a cat toy.

ANONYMOUS

———————•••———————

She wailed and screamed and
howled... She got down and
cried under the door so that
we could hear her better.

DOREEN TOVEY

Any household with at least
one feline member has no
need for an alarm clock.

LOUISE A. BELCHER

•●•

A cat determined not to be found
can fold itself up like a pocket
handkerchief if it wants to.

LOUIS J. CAMUTI

•●•

The cat who looks poorly and sad
has just stolen a carton of cream
and is about to be sick in the hall.

ANONYMOUS

A creature that never cries
over spilt milk: a cat.

EVAN ESAR

We need a word for all the
kitty-prints that are all
over my windshield.

MEGAN COUGHLIN

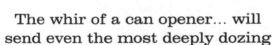

The whir of a can opener... will
send even the most deeply dozing
cat bounding into the kitchen.

BARBARA L. DIAMOND

Most cats, when they are out
want to be in, and vice versa,
and often simultaneously.

LOUIS J. CAMUTI

———————•●•———————

The minute they think you are
not looking, a cat acts like a fool.

K. C. BUFFINGTON

CAT CRAZY

Mad Cat Man is a less widely reported phenomenon [than Mad Cat Lady], but I am here to tell you that he exists.

TOM COX

Some people have cats and
go on to lead normal lives.

ANONYMOUS

Mimi slept not only indoors, but
in Father Adams's armchair, on
his corduroy waistcoat which he
took off specially for her each
night before he went to bed.

DOREEN TOVEY

Everyone's pet is the
most outstanding.

JEAN COCTEAU

There is, incidentally, no way of talking about cats that enables one to come off as a sane person.

DAN GREENBURG

───────●●●───────

Cats have an infallible understanding of total concentration – and get between you and it.

ARTHUR BRIDGES

───────●●●───────

The extraordinary thing about *any* cat is the effect it has on its owner.

PETER GETHERS

Do our cats name us? My former
husband swore that Humphrey
and Dolly and Bean Blossom
called me The Big Hamburger.

ELEANORA WALKER

———●●●———

It doesn't do to be sentimental
about cats; the best ones
don't respect you for it.

SUSAN HOWATCH

———●●●———

I have noticed that what cats most
appreciate in a human being is...
his or her entertainment value.

GEOFFREY HOUSEHOLD

Don't let anyone tell
you loving a cat is silly.
Love, in any form, is a
precious commodity.

BARBARA L. DIAMOND

CATS WILL TAKE
A MESSAGE

A cat will do what it
wants when it wants,
and there's not a thing
you can do about it.

FRANK PERKINS

The cat is the only animal which
accepts the comforts but rejects
the bondage of domesticity.

GEORGES LOUIS LECLERC

Cats pride themselves on
their ability to do nothing.

JOHN R. F. BREEN

Cats are connoisseurs of comfort.

JAMES HERRIOT

I would like to see anyone...
persuade a thousand cats to do
anything at the same time.

NEIL GAIMAN

———————•••———————

A cat doesn't 'roll' well with a
change of someone else's making.

CAROLE WILBOURN

———————•••———————

Cats were put into the world to
disprove the dogma that all things
were created to serve man.

PAUL GRAY

When addressed, a gentleman
cat does not move a muscle. He
looks as if he hasn't heard.

MAY SARTON

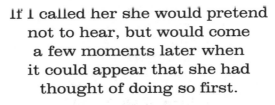

If I called her she would pretend
not to hear, but would come
a few moments later when
it could appear that she had
thought of doing so first.

ARTHUR WEIGALL

Cats are successful
underachievers.

JIM AITES

A cat sees no good reason why
it should obey another animal,
even if it does stand on two legs.

SARAH THOMPSON

The idea of calm exists
in a sitting cat.

JULES RENARD

HAVING KITTENS

If only cats grew
into kittens.

ROBERT A. M. STERN

Kittens are angels with whiskers.

ANONYMOUS

● ● ●

Kittens believe that all nature is occupied with their diversion.

FRANÇOIS-AUGUSTIN DE PARADIS DE MONCRIF

● ● ●

A kitten is the most irresistible comedian in the world. Its wide-open eyes gleam with wonder and mirth.

AGNES REPPLIER

No matter how much cats
fight, there always seems
to be plenty of kittens.

ABRAHAM LINCOLN

—————•●•—————

An ordinary kitten will ask more
questions than any five-year-old.

CARL VAN VECHTEN

They say the test
of literary power is
whether a man can
write an inscription.
I say 'Can he
name a kitten?'

SAMUEL BUTLER

It is impossible to keep a
straight face in the presence
of one or more kittens.

CYNTHIA E. VARNADO

Who would believe such pleasure
from a wee ball o' fur?

IRISH PROVERB

A cat with kittens nearly
always decides sooner or
later to move them.

SIDNEY DENHAM

CAT HABITS

Cats invented
self-esteem.

ERMA BOMBECK

The cat, which is a solitary
beast, is single-minded
and goes its way alone.

H. G. WELLS

———●●●———

All cats, given the opportunity,
are people-watchers.

ROGER CARAS

———●●●———

A cat is an example of
sophistication minus civilization.

ANONYMOUS

A cat is never vulgar.

CARL VAN VECHTEN

———•●•———

When he moved, he didn't limp
like any ordinary, normal cat,
he went round in anguished,
three-legged leaps like a frog.

DOREEN TOVEY

———•●•———

Some animals are secretive;
some are shy. A cat is private.

LEONARD MICHAELS

Among animals, cats
are the top-hatted,
frock-coated statesmen
going about their affairs
at their own pace.

ROBERT STEARNS

Rarely do you see a cat
discomfited. They have no
conscience, and they never regret.
Maybe we secretly envy them.

BARBARA WEBSTER

—•—•—

It's very hard to be polite
if you're a cat.

ANONYMOUS

—•—•—

Few animals display their
mood via facial expressions
as distinctly as cats.

KONRAD LORENZ

It is remarkable, in cats, that the outer life they reveal to their masters is one of perpetual confident boredom.

ROBLEY WILSON

TOP CATS

Cats are kindly masters,
just so long as you
remember your place.

PAUL GRAY

You are my cat and I
am your human.

HILAIRE BELLOC

The cat does not offer services.
The cat offers itself.

WILLIAM S. BURROUGHS

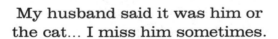

My husband said it was him or
the cat... I miss him sometimes.

ANONYMOUS

The phrase 'domestic
cat' is an oxymoron.

GEORGE WILL

———•••———

My dog thinks he's human...
My cat thinks he's God.

ANONYMOUS

———•••———

The mathematical probability
of a common cat doing exactly
as it pleases is the one scientific
absolute in the world.

LYNN M. OSBAND

Of all God's creatures,
there is only one that
cannot be made the
slave of the lash.
That one is the cat.

MARK TWAIN

Cats can be cooperative when
something feels good.

ROGER CARAS

———•●•———

Coming in second best,
especially to someone as poorly
coordinated as a human being,
grates their sensibility.

STEPHEN BAKER

———•●•———

Cats only pretend to be
domesticated if they think there's
a bowl of milk in it for them.

ROBIN WILLIAMS

WILD THING

Prowling his own quiet
backyard or asleep
by the fire, he is still
only a whisker away
from the wilds.

JEAN BURDEN

Lat take a cat, and foster
hym wel with milk
And tender flessh, and
make his couche of silk,
And lat hym seen a
mous go by the wal,
Anon he weyveth milk
and flessh and al,
And every deyntee that
is in that hous,
Swich appetit hath he
to ete a mous.

GEOFFREY CHAUCER, *THE MANCIPLE'S TALE*

—•●•—

It is in the nature of cats
to do a certain amount of
unescorted roaming.

ADLAI STEVENSON

When all candles be out,
all cats be grey.

JOHN HEYWOOD

———•••———

The cat of the slums and alleys,
starved, outcast, harried...
still displays the self-reliant
watchfulness which man has
never taught it to lay aside.

SAKI

———•••———

The cat is the only animal
without visible means of
support who still manages to
earn a living in the city.

CARL VAN VECHTEN

The cat is a wild animal that
inhabits the homes of humans.

KONRAD LORENZ

———•●•———

After dark all cats are leopards.

NATIVE AMERICAN PROVERB

———•●•———

Cat: a pygmy lion who
loves mice, hates dogs and
patronises human beings.

OLIVER HERFORD

The wildest of all the wild animals
was the Cat. He walked by himself,
and all places were alike to him.

RUDYARD KIPLING

• • •

They get the exact same look
on their face whether they see
a moth or an axe-murderer.

PAULA POUNDSTONE

THE WRITER'S MEWS

A catless writer is
almost inconceivable.

BARBARA HOLLAND

What greater gift than
the love of a cat?

CHARLES DICKENS

———•●•———

If you want to be a psychological
novelist... the best thing you
can do is own a pair of cats.

ALDOUS HUXLEY

———•●•———

Our perfect companions never
have fewer than four feet.

COLETTE

Cats are dangerous
companions for
writers because
cat-watching is a
near-perfect method
of writing avoidance.

DAN GREENBURG

Poets generally love cats –
because poets have no delusions
about their own superiority.

MARION GARRETTY

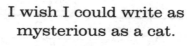

I wish I could write as
mysterious as a cat.

EDGAR ALLAN POE

Because of our willingness to
accept cats as superhuman
creatures, they are the
ideal animals with which
to work creatively.

RONI SCHOTTER

A cat has absolute emotional honesty... People hide their feelings for various reasons, but cats never do.

ERNEST HEMINGWAY

———— •●• ————

Authors are sometimes like tomcats: They distrust all the other toms but they are kind to kittens.

MALCOLM COWLEY

———— •●• ————

Authors like cats because they are such quiet, lovable, wise creatures, and cats like authors for the same reasons.

ROBERTSON DAVIES

WHY WE LOVE CATS

Like children, cats
exist on a separate
and probably higher
plane than we do.

PETER GETHERS

His friendship is not easily won
but it is something worth having.

M. K. JOSEPH

———————— •●• ————————

In the middle of a world that
has always been a bit mad, the
cat walks with confidence.

ROSANNE AMBERSON

———————— •●• ————————

There is something about the
presence of a cat… that seems to
take the bite out of being alone.

LOUIS J. CAMUTI

People who love cats have some
of the biggest hearts around.

SUSAN EASTERLY

———•●•———

Our character is what God
and cats know of us.

THOMAS PAINE

———•●•———

He lives in the half-lights in
secret places, free and alone – this
mysterious little great being...

MARGARET BENSON

Who among us hasn't envied a cat's ability to ignore the cares of daily life and to relax completely?

KAREN BRADEMEYER

As each person reached to pet him, he rubbed his tiny head against her hand and purred.

VICKI MYRON

Cats at firesides live luxuriously and are the picture of comfort.

LEIGH HUNT

She sat there on the hearthrug...
her eyes screwed tight with
anticipation, her paws pounding
up and down like little pistons.

DOREEN TOVEY

———— •●• ————

By the time my key hits the lock
I hear the soft press of paws
on the other side of the door.

GWEN COOPER

———— •●• ————

Has anyone ever had a stroke
or a heart attack while cosied
up with a pet? I doubt it.

ROBERT BRAULT

THE CAT CONUNDRUM

If you would know
what a cat is thinking
about, you must hold
its paw in your hand
for a long time.

CHAMPFLEURY

A cat is a puzzle
for which there
is no solution.

HAZEL NICHOLSON

The cat is domestic only as far as suits its own ends.

SAKI

———•••———

[Cat names] give one a certain degree more confidence that the animal belongs to you.

ALAN AYCKBOURN

———•••———

The way to keep a cat is to try to chase it away.

EDGAR WATSON HOWE

The only mystery about the cat is why it ever decided to become a domestic animal.

COMPTON MACKENZIE

———●●●———

The trouble with cats is that they've got no tact.

P. G. WODEHOUSE

———●●●———

Cats come and go without ever leaving.

MARTHA CURTIS

If stretching were wealth,
the cat would be rich.

AFRICAN PROVERB

———●●———

People that don't like cats
haven't met the right one yet.

DEBORAH A. EDWARDS

CAUTIONARY TAILS

[I am] a dog man, and all felines can tell this at a glance – a sharp, vindictive glance.

JAMES THURBER

I was only a small child when
the seeds of cat enchantment
were sown within me.

MAY EUSTACE

———————•●•———————

A cat would check to see if you
brought anything to eat, and if
not, would turn and walk away.

MIKE DUPREE

———————•●•———————

They can do all sorts of
amazing things like hiding in
the tiniest room imaginable
and refusing to be found...

PETER GETHERS

Another cat I knew fancied
shrimps in the bath as a pick-
me-up... But nobody was allowed
to watch him while he ate.

DOREEN TOVEY

⎯⎯●●⎯⎯

She clawed her way into my
heart and wouldn't let go.

MISSY ALTIJD

⎯⎯●●⎯⎯

Never wear anything
that panics the cat.

P. J. O'ROURKE

To assume a cat's asleep is a grave
mistake. He can close his eyes
and keep both his ears awake.

AILEEN FISHER

———●●———

Always the cat remains a little
beyond the limits we try to set
for him in our blind folly.

ANDRE NORTON

FURBALLS

Whether they be
the musician cats in
my band or the real
cats of the world,
they all got style.

RAY CHARLES

I really am a cat transformed
into a woman... I purr, I scratch,
and sometimes I bite.

BRIGITTE BARDOT

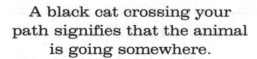

A black cat crossing your
path signifies that the animal
is going somewhere.

GROUCHO MARX

It doesn't matter whether
a cat is black or white, so
long as it catches mice.

DENG XIAOPING

No animal should ever jump up
on the dining room furniture
unless... he can hold his
own in the conversation.

FRAN LEBOWITZ

If a cat washes her face,
there will be visitors.

JAPANESE PROVERB

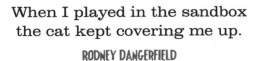

When I played in the sandbox
the cat kept covering me up.

RODNEY DANGERFIELD

What happens if you
strap buttered toast
to the back of a cat?

STEVEN WRIGHT

You can visualise a hundred
cats. Beyond that, you can't.
Two hundred, five hundred,
it all looks the same.

JACK WRIGHT, THE GUINNESS WORLD RECORD HOLDER
FOR OWNING THE MOST CATS AT ONE TIME (689)

Never play cat and mouse
games if you're a mouse.

DON ADDIS

The man who carries a cat by
the tail learns something that
can be learned in no other way.

MARK TWAIN

Cats, I think, live out
their lives fulfilling
their expectations.

IRVING TOWNSEND

If you're interested in finding out more about our books, find us on Facebook at **Summersdale Publishers** and follow us on Twitter at **@Summersdale**.

www.summersdale.com